Carlos Alcaraz

Carlos Alcaraz

Rachael Hanel

Living in THE SPOTLIGHT

CREATIVE EDUCATION
CREATIVE PAPERBACKS

Published by Creative Education and Creative Paperbacks
P.O. Box 227, Mankato, Minnesota 56002
Creative Education and Creative Paperbacks are imprints
of The Creative Company
www.thecreativecompany.us

Book design by Blue Design (www.bluedes.com)
Art direction by Tom Morgan

Images by Dreamstime/Antonio Lopez Velasco, 10, Antonio Ros, 23, Filedimage, 2, 33, Zhukovsky, 9; Getty Images/ADRIAN DENNIS, 30–31, Clive Brunskill, 38, Eduardo MunozAlvarez/VIEWpress, 26, EMMANUEL DUNAND, 14, FREDERIC J. BROWN, 45, JOSE JORDAN, 19, Leonardo Gerzon/NurPhoto, 41, Manuel Romano/NurPhoto, 13, MAURO PIMENTEL, 25, MICHAEL ERREY, 20, OSCAR DEL POZO, 29, Oscar J. Barroso / Europa Press Sports, 17, Tim Clayton-Corbis, cover; Wikimedia Commons/Barcex, 46, Daniel Cooper, 4–5, Like tears in rain, cover, 6–7, 34, 37, Yannick JAMOT, 44

Library of Congress Cataloging-in-Publication Data
Names: Hanel, Rachael author
Title: Carlos Alcaraz / by Rachael Hanel.
Description: Mankato, Minnesota : Creative Education and Creative Paperbacks, [2026] | Series: Living in the Spotlight | Includes bibliographical references and index. | Audience: Ages 10-14 | Audience: Grades 7-9 | Summary: "Get to know Spanish tennis prodigy Carlos Alcaraz in this sports biography that showcases his athletic achievements, personal challenges, and personal life. Written for middle-grade readers, it includes table of contents, sidebars, glossary, resources, and index"– Provided by publisher.
Identifiers: LCCN 2025021171 (print) | LCCN 2025021172 (ebook) | ISBN 9798895811283 library binding | ISBN 9798896800811 paperback | ISBN 9798895812549 ebook
Subjects: LCSH: Alcaraz, Carlos Garfia, 2003- | Australian Open (Tennis tournament)–History | Internationaux de France de tennis, Roland Garros–History | Wimbledon Championships–History | U.S. Open (Tennis tournament)–History | Tennis players–Spain–Biography | Fathers and sons–Spain | LCGFT: Biographies
Classification: LCC GV994.A46 H36 2026 (print) | LCC GV994.A46 (ebook) | DDC 796.342092 [B]–dc23/eng/20250717
LC record available at https://lccn.loc.gov/2025021171
LC ebook record available at https://lccn.loc.gov/2025021172

Printed in the United States

CONTENTS

Introduction

In June 2024, Carlos Alcaraz, 21, the reigning Wimbledon champion, was down two sets to one to Germany's Alexander Zverev at the French Open. Alcaraz, ranked third, had two Grand Slam Championships under his belt. But Zverev, ranked second in the Association of Tennis Professionals (ATP), had won more than 20 career titles. He also had more years of playing tennis than Alcaraz.

But Alcaraz came back strong in the second set, handing Zverev a 6–1 loss. The two battled back and forth in the fifth set: 1–1, Alcaraz 2–1, Alcaraz 3–1. The Spaniard put his finger behind his ear, wanting to hear the roar of the fans. He drummed up more fan applause with his racket, lifting it up, down, up, down.

Zverev 2–3. Alcaraz 4–2. Alcaraz 5–2.

Alcaraz needed one more game to win the title. He served. Zverev **backhanded** it in return. Alcaraz powered it back. Zverev **forehanded** it into the net. The game was finally over. Alcaraz fell to the clay in relief and celebration. He won the 2024 French Open!

The win for Alcaraz was his first French Open title and third Grand Slam Championship. The win made him the youngest man to win a Grand Slam on three different playing surfaces: clay, grass, and hard court. But he didn't just walk onto a court and win. Alcaraz had trained for more than 15 years. He practiced through pain and fatigue and doubts. Yet he always stayed focused on his goal: to become one of the best tennis players ever.

Murcia is one of the largest cities in Spain. It is made up of 54 districts, El Palmar being one of the largest.

CHAPTER 1:

It Runs in the Family

Carlos Alcaraz was born on May 5, 2003, in the town of El Palmar, Spain. The town is in southeastern Spain, not far from the coast of the Mediterranean Sea. Alcaraz was the second of four sons born to his parents, Carlos Alcaraz González and Virginia Garfia Escandón. His brothers are Álvaro, Sergio, and Jaime.

Alcaraz's father was the athletic director of a local tennis and swimming club in nearby Murcia. The Alcaraz family had long-standing ties to the club. The club had been founded in 1923 as a hunting club. Those who could afford it went there and paid to shoot pigeons. Alcaraz's grandfather, also named Carlos, decided to add a swimming pool and tennis courts to the club.

Instead of hard courts, Grandpa Carlos chose to install red clay on the 13 courts. Red clay was more expensive, but tennis players in that part of Spain enjoyed playing on a clay surface. The club soon earned the reputation for having the best clay courts in the area. Today the club is still known as Tiro de Pichón, or Pigeon Strike, which recalls the club's early days as a place for hunters.

Alcaraz's father bought his young son, nicknamed Carlitos, a tennis racket when he was four years old. Alcaraz started to play at his father's club. He dreamed of becoming a tennis star. His uncle, Tomás, took little Alcaraz to play in his first tennis tournament when he was only five years old. At the tournament, it was clear the child had a great talent for the sport. He competed against an opponent who was a few years older and taller than Alcaraz. These young boys didn't use a **depressurized** tennis ball like boys that age usually did. They used an adult ball. Every time the ball bounced, it flew over Alcaraz's head. He lost the first set. He realized he had to move into the **forecourt**. This allowed him to **volley** every shot instead of letting it bounce. He didn't win the match, but it was close. Alcaraz displayed impressive skill and the ability to adapt, which would come in handy years later.

One of Alcaraz's first coaches was Kiko Navarro. One day, Navarro was at Alcaraz's father's club and Alcaraz Sr. asked Navarro to watch his son play. Alcaraz was only four or five, but Navarro

Alcaraz faces Frederico Ferreira Silva at the ATP Challenger L'Aquila in August 2019.

LISINI
RUZIONI
CARTOLERIA
ARROSTICIN
DIVINI
LCESTRUZZI
IFER CELIPREM
NARDO
MAURIZIO
• PROGETTAZIONE •
EMPORIOARREDAMENTI
UNIREST

ZOOM IN: LIKE FATHER, LIKE BROTHER

Alcaraz's father, Carlos Alcaraz González, was a professional tennis player. He reached a career-high No. 963 world ranking in 1990 and played professionally through 2005. But he couldn't afford to keep playing. He founded the Carlos Alcaraz Tennis Academy by Reina in 1993. Today, Alcaraz Sr. and his staff run schools, competitions, and camps. His son (and Alcaraz's brother), Álvaro, is on the staff at the academy. Alvaro works with the competition teams and is a national tennis trainer. Alvaro also travels with his brother and is at his side for his biggest wins and hardest losses.

spotted the child's talent. Navarro noticed that he was small, but his hand-eye coordination and speed came naturally. Because Alcaraz Sr. had to run the tennis club and raise his other sons, Navarro became Alcaraz's main coach.

Coaching a young player involved more than just showing him how to move and hit the ball. Coach Navarro also had to help Alcaraz focus. For example, he wouldn't let him play video games or have a cell phone. That focus would soon pay off. Alcaraz was playing well enough to qualify for tournaments. However, traveling required money. The Alcaraz family did not have enough money to send their son to tournaments.

The family tried to find **sponsors**. Alfonso Lopez Rueda, a local businessman, played tennis at the same club as little Alcaraz. He noticed how well the young boy played and became friendly with the family. He agreed to send Alcaraz to his first tournament. Lopez Rueda loaned the family 2,000 euros ($2,075 USD) from his company, the dessert manufacturer Postres Reina. At the Under-10 World Tennis Championship in Pula, Croatia, Alcaraz reached the final against Daniel Rincón, a fellow Spaniard.

Even though Alcaraz did well, his temper was hard to control. In tournaments, he would get angry and throw his rackets. If he lost a match, he'd cry and wouldn't leave the court. Navarro would walk away and just let him cry. Alcaraz didn't like losing at anything, whether it be cards, board games, or padel—a racket sport played indoors.

Fortunately, Alcaraz played tennis so well that he won more than he lost. After the trip to Croatia, Postres Reina started to pay for his trips to competitions around Spain and Europe. He got a big sponsor when he was about 10 years old. At the Barcelona trophy presentation, he was wearing a new Rolex gold watch, worth about $35,000. This was just the beginning of big sponsorships to come.

When Alcaraz was 13, he took another big step toward tennis success. He signed a contract with International Management Group (IMG), a sports management company. Manager Albert Molina had spent weeks watching Alcaraz in tournaments. The contract came with more sponsors: Lotto, a clothing company, and Babolat, a racket company. Postres Reina continued to sponsor him, too. Alcaraz realized he had a shot to become an elite tennis

ZOOM IN: SPANISH IDOL

When Alcaraz was first learning to play tennis, he had another tennis player from Spain to look up to: Rafael Nadal. About the time Alcaraz played in his first tournament, Nadal won his fifth career Grand Slam title at Wimbledon in 2008. That same year he won a gold medal at the Olympic Games in Beijing. When Alcaraz grew up and faced his idol for the first time, it was at the Madrid Open on May 5, 2021, Alcaraz's 18th birthday. Alcaraz called it "kind of a nightmare." But he also added that "it was a privilege to share the court" with Nadal.

Alcaraz plays against fellow tennis legend Rafael Nadal at the Madrid Open on May 5, 2021.

player. His tantrums started to fade as he matured and realized how much was at stake.

The sponsorships gave Alcaraz access to the top tournaments in Europe. And the contract with IMG led Alcaraz to his next coach, the former number one-ranked tennis player in the world, Juan Carlos Ferrero. The young teen was well on his way to success, though the path would not be without setbacks. How well he would handle those setbacks would be the real test for Alcaraz.

Coach Ferrero lends his tennis wisdom to a young Alcaraz.

CHAPTER 2:

A Taste of Success

To work with Coach Ferrero, Alcaraz had to move to Villena, about an hour away from his home, to attend the Juan Carlos Ferrero Training Academy. He would get to work with a top coach and learn from the other players that Ferrero coached.

It was 2018. Alcaraz was just 15 years old. He and his family realized it would be a tough sacrifice, but working with Ferrero would be worth it. If he wanted to compete in Grand Slam tournaments with the best of the best, he needed the finest coach he could find. Coach Navarro had taken Alcaraz as far as he could go. He was ready to hand the young star off to a new coach. Navarro continued to coach young players at Alcaraz's father's club in El Palmar as Alcaraz moved on.

At the academy, Alcaraz's tennis skills impressed Ferrero. He knew the young man was something special. In 2023 he told *Vogue* magazine that when he started

MAPFRE
Babolat

ZOOM IN: WHAT ARE THE GRAND SLAMS?

Four major tennis tournaments are known as the "Grand Slams." These tournaments are the Australian Open, French Open, Wimbledon, and U.S. Open. The tournaments are the most famous ones and offer the most prize money. Every tennis player dreams of achieving a career grand slam—that is, winning each tournament at least once over a career. As of early 2025, Alcaraz is just one win away from completing a career Grand Slam. The tournaments got the name from a term in the card game of contract bridge. In the game, it means winning all possible tricks. Alcaraz's rival, Djokovic, holds the record for winning the most grand slam tournaments: 24.

Alcaraz at the Australian Open in January 2022.

training Alcaraz, Alcaraz "was doing a lot of different things—drop shots and lobs and running to the net, things that young kids don't do."

From 2017 to 2020, Alcaraz competed in junior International Tennis Federation (ITF) Tour tournaments. The junior ITF is for players under 18. It's a training ground for young players who want to play professionally as adults.

His strong skills of agility, speed, and intelligence on the court continued to impress his opponents and audiences. Anyone who saw him play realized he was going to be a remarkable pro tennis player, perhaps even one of the best. In the junior ITF tournaments, Alcaraz had a combined 46 wins and 16 losses.

Alcaraz had a major victory at age 15. He played in the ATP Challenger Tour in Alicante, Spain. This tour is a stepping stone to the professional ATP tournaments. In Alicante, Alcaraz beat Jannik Sinner, who had just won the Next Gen ATP Finals. This gave Alcaraz a lot of confidence. Alcaraz won multiple tournaments on the Challenger **circuit**. Only 12 players under the age of 17 have ever won multiple Challenger tournaments. These included tennis stars Nadal and Novak Djokovic.

Alcaraz also competed in the 2019 Junior Wimbledon tournament, giving him a taste of what it would be like to compete on a Grand Slam court. He made it to the quarterfinals. Alcaraz's record in junior tournaments between 2017 and 2019 was 46–16.

Despite the hectic travel schedule, Alcaraz tried as much as possible to live a normal teenage life. He received tutoring at Ferrero's academy. But on longer breaks back home, he took classes at his local high school. Most weekends he returned home to spend quality time with his parents and three brothers.

But his focus was tennis. On January 6, 2020, Alcaraz achieved a career-high ITF junior ranking at No. 22. This made him the highest-ranked 16-year-old in the world. The tennis world started to buzz with news of this up-and-coming youngster from Spain. He started to earn comparisons to his hero, fellow Spaniard Nadal. His family, coaches, and Alcaraz himself had high hopes for the future.

"I believe I can reach No. 1 in the world. That's my dream," Alcaraz said in an interview with Trans World Sport in January 2020.

Soon after, he qualified to play in ATP adult tournaments. Now he was playing with the big boys, players he had admired as a young child. In February 2020, at the age of 16, Alcaraz made his ATP

Alcaraz at the ATP Challenger Tour in September 2020.

NIKE
NIKE

debut at the Rio Open in Brazil. This tournament was a big deal. It would show Alcaraz whether he could compete against players who were older than him and who had much more experience. At the Rio Open, Alcaraz won the wildcard singles draw, which allowed him into the tournament despite his low ranking of No. 406 in the world.

His first opponent was the No. 41 ranked Albert Ramos-Vinolas, who was also from Spain. This was the first time Alcaraz faced a player ranked in the top 100 in the world. But he was not frightened. Alcaraz started strong, winning the opening set 7–6. He also started strong in the second set, but Ramos-Vinolas battled back to win 6–4. This forced a deciding match. Ramos-Vinolas raced to a 4–0 lead. Alcaraz wasn't done. He came back with a five-game run, spending most of his time and fierce energy on the **baseline**. At the final-set **tiebreak** and fourth **match point**, Ramos-Vinolas sent a **forehand** into the net. Alcaraz won his first-round match at 3 a.m. They had played for three hours and 37 minutes. Unfortunately, his next opponent from Argentina, Federico Coria, didn't let Alcaraz advance to the quarterfinals. Coria proved to be the better player with a 6–4, 4–6, 6–4 win over the young Alcaraz.

ZOOM IN: HOW TO SCORE A TENNIS MATCH

Tennis is unlike other sports, in which points add up one by one. A tennis match is made up of games and sets. In a game, if a player fails to get the ball over the net, the other player earns a point. Points are scored as follows: 0 points = love; 1 point = 15; 2 points = 30; 3 points = 40. In order to win a game, a player must earn four points. A player must win six games, by at least two games, to win a set. If there's a tie, or a player reaches six and is only up by one, the tiebreak rules become complicated. In most tournaments, a player needs to win three out of five sets in order to win the match.

16-year-old Alcaraz at the Rio Open, 2020.

Still, Alcaraz knew his first tournament as a professional was a success. He went into it as a major **underdog**, but still won his first match. This gave him a huge boost of confidence. After the tournament he said, "I will remember Rio forever."

Alcaraz was sure to remember Rio for more than one reason: this was the last tournament he'd play for a long while. An unknown virus was about to sweep the world. It would bring tournament play to a grinding halt.

CHAPTER 3:

Reaching No. 1

Just as Alcaraz was hitting his stride on the world's biggest courts, the COVID-19 **pandemic** swept across the world. Officials shut down in-person gatherings in hopes of keeping people safe from the deadly disease. The virus halted all tournaments well into the summer of 2020. This forced Alcaraz and other players to take a break from competitions. For a young player used to a busy travel schedule, this was a make-or-break moment. Could Alcaraz still stay sharp without competing? Or would the time off set him back?

Alcaraz used the time to get stronger. At the Ferrero Academy, he hit the gym. When Ferrero first started to coach Alcaraz, he said the boy was like spaghetti: "Very thin. No muscles at all. Not in the back, not in the legs." Intense focus at the gym during this time off helped Alcaraz build muscle.

Alcaraz at the 2022 U.S. Open in New York City.

Alcaraz putting in the work at the 2021 ATP Tour Madrid Open.

Alcaraz also worked on more technical aspects of his game that needed improvement. When play resumed in late 2020, Alcaraz was stronger than ever. He continued to rack up wins on the Challenger circuit.

In January 2021, Alcaraz finally reached one of his dreams: to play in a Grand Slam tournament. He made his Grand Slam debut at the Australian Open. In the first round, Alcaraz beat a virtual unknown in just 25 minutes. He lost in the second round, but making it to the second round in his Grand Slam debut was a huge accomplishment.

Better yet, he cracked the top 100, a major milestone for any professional player. He was ranked No. 94—and he had just turned 18. Comparisons to Nadal continued. Nadal was also a teenager when he broke into the top 100.

On May 5, 2021, for the first time, Alcaraz faced Nadal on the court. It was the second round of the Madrid Open. The two Spaniards were playing in Spain in front of cheering home crowds. Not surprising, the much more experienced Nadal soundly defeated Alcaraz 1–6, 2–6.

Alcaraz wouldn't let the loss get him down. In 2021, Alcaraz participated in all four major Grand Slam tournaments. In the French Open he made it to the third round. At Wimbledon, he lost in the second round. He performed his best at the U.S. Open, making it all the way to the quarterfinals, where he lost to Felix Auger-Aliassime.

Alcaraz returns the ball to Italy's Jannik Sinner, Wimbledon 2022.

By May 2022, he was now ranked in the top 10. He had just won two major tournaments: the Barcelona Open and the Rio Open. But in many ways, he was still a teenager. After winning the Barcelona Open, he went straight to the swimming pool at the back of the club and dove in, still in his shorts and shirt. Soon he was joined by dozens of fellow teens—the ball boys and ball girls. They all laughed—especially the tournament's champion.

On his 19th birthday, May 5, 2022, he once again faced Nadal in the Madrid Open. It was the quarterfinals. This time Alcaraz won 6–2, 1–6, 6–3. He went on to win the entire tournament.

In September, Alcaraz played in the U.S. Open. It was an exhausting tournament with many long, hard-fought matches. He endured a five-hour, 15-minute quarterfinal match with Sinner. His semifinal match over Frances Tiafoe lasted more than four hours. In the final, he faced Norwegian Casper Ruud. Across seven matches at the U.S. Open, Alcaraz was on the court for 23 hours and 40 minutes. It was his first major tournament title. Alcaraz was the first teenager since Pete Sampras in 1990 to win the U.S. Open.

In addition to the win, he added another honor to his growing resume: a number one ranking. Alcaraz was 19 years, 4 months, and 6 days old when he became the youngest male tennis player to be ranked number one.

In between playing in one of the world's most exclusive tournaments for tennis pros, Alcaraz was finishing up his last year of high school online. When at home, he loved hanging out with his

ZOOM IN: SHOW ME THE MONEY

Alcaraz is successful and has a huge fan base. Because of this, many companies pay Alcaraz to promote their brands. They think that his fans will want to buy the same brands that Alcaraz promotes. So far, Alcaraz is one of the faces of Nike, Louis Vuitton, Rolex, BMW, Calvin Klein, and others. The financial details of these deals are private. Experts can only estimate how much money Alcaraz is making through sponsors. But some think he has earned between $200 and $300 million through brand **endorsements**. Compare that to the $40 million he has won in his lifetime through tournament wins.

Clay courts are Alcaraz's favorite type of court.

friends, jet skiing, watching soccer, listening to music, and watching movies (*Rocky* is one of his favorites). Family and friends were truly Alcaraz's support system. He would need this support when things did not go his way on the court.

In May 2023, Alcaraz endured one of his worst losses. In the third round of the Italian Open, he lost to a virtual unknown. Fabian Marozsan, a Hungarian, was only ranked No. 135. And his game against Alcaraz was only Marozsan's second ATP match ever. Alcaraz took the defeat in stride. He complimented Marozsan's play and said he just did not feel comfortable. "It was tough for me to get into the match," Alcaraz said. The defeat may have actually been for the best, because it allowed Alcaraz to rest before the major summer tournaments, like Wimbledon.

At Wimbledon that year, Alcaraz faced Djokovic, a major rival. Djokovic was looking for his fifth consecutive Wimbledon win. The match started out poorly for Alcaraz. He did not look confident. His normally strong forehand was nowhere to be found. He lost that set 1–6. The second set went to Alcaraz, who found his rhythm. The set game was intense: strong volleys back-and-forth. Djokovic was moving quickly to the tiebreak. But Alcaraz kept fighting. He hung on to get the tiebreak and won the set 7–6 (6). By the third set, the match had been going on for two hours. Both players vowed to remain strong. The third set went to Alcaraz 6–1. After that set, Djokovic went to the locker room to change clothes and regroup. He returned looking strong and won the fourth set. In the fifth set, when it was clear Alcaraz would win, Djokovic became frustrated. He smashed his racket. Alcaraz stayed cool. He went on to win the set and the Wimbledon championship. He now had two major tournament titles under his belt. And he was only 20 years old.

Alcaraz was at the top of his game. But would it last?

ZOOM IN: RED CLAY COURTS

There are four types of tennis courts: hard-surface, grass, clay, and carpet. In the United States, most tennis players learn to play on hard-surface courts. These courts might be a mixture of asphalt and concrete. But in other parts of the world, like Europe, red clay courts are most common. At the same time, they are more challenging to play on. That's because tennis balls move more slowly on clay. They also bounce higher. A player needs a lot of stamina to play on clay. The French Open is an example of a tournament played on a red clay court. Luckily for Alcaraz, he grew up playing on red clay and has an advantage over others who did not.

CHAPTER 4:

New Dreams to Chase

Alcaraz was far from done earning major tournament titles. In 2024, he won the French Open (also known as Roland Garros). That year he added another Wimbledon title. This was his second Wimbledon win in a row.

Though he was tired after Wimbledon, Alcaraz had very little time to prepare for his next big moment: the 2024 Olympics. He dreamed of adding a gold medal to his growing list of accomplishments.

At the Olympic games, Alcaraz blasted his opponents on his way to making the final. So did his rival, Djokovic. Djokovic was 37 years old and had already played in four previous Olympic games. But he had never won gold. He wanted to finally earn that shiny top medal.

Alcaraz faces his rival Djokovic at the 2024 Paris Olympics.

ZOOM IN: A FITTING TRIBUTE

If you go to the elementary school that Alcaraz attended in Murcia, Spain, you will see his face painted on an outside wall. It's a young Carlos, or "Carlitos" as he was known as a boy. Another, much larger, mural of Alcaraz can be found on Calle Mota Reguerón, where you would enter El Palmar, his hometown. The artist Sbah completed the mural in just eight days. The art shows Alcaraz delivering his famous backhand. Alcaraz himself attended the dedication of the mural on June 6, 2022. There he said, "I'm very proud to represent the Murcia region and bring the name of El Palmar to every corner of the world."

On August 4, the much-anticipated match began. The two men had just faced each other at the Wimbledon final. But at Wimbledon, Djokovic was still recovering from knee surgery and was not playing 100 percent. Now, a few weeks later, he was much stronger. The two had come to Paris to give it their all.

Djokovic won the first game in the first set, but Alcaraz tied it. After Djokovic was up 2–1, Alcaraz tied it again. After an incredible serve at break point, Djokovic was up again 3-2. Then it was tied 4–4. Then again at 6–6. When Djokovic reached out to stop a fast forehand from Alcaraz, it eased back into Alcaraz's court, but he was too far back. Djokovic, the master of the tiebreak, won the first set 7–6 (3). It took more than 90 minutes.

Djokovic won the first game of the second set. His serves averaged 118 miles (190 kilometers) per hour. But Alcaraz was serving up to 122 miles (197 kilometers) per hour. Soon it was tied 2–2. This set, too, was back-and-forth. Alcaraz was fighting hard. But it was not enough. Again, Djokovic's strength in the tiebreak showed through. He won the second set, 7–6 (2) to claim his first gold medal. (Unlike in regular tennis tournaments, the Olympic games use a best-

Alcaraz is one of the most dedicated up-and-coming tennis stars we will see for many years to come.

of-three-set format.) The match had lasted nearly three hours. Had Alcaraz won, he would have been the youngest male tennis player to win gold. But surely, he has many more Olympic games ahead of him.

Just three weeks later, Alcaraz returned to the U.S. Open, hoping to gain another major tournament title. But it was not to be. He was exhausted. The intense Olympic match wore him out physically and mentally. He lost in straight sets to Dutch player Botic van de Zandschulp in the second round.

But soon, Alcaraz regained his strength. He came back to win the China Open in October. In January 2025, he again faced Djokovic, this time in the quarterfinals of the Australian Open. Djokovic outlasted Alcaraz to win the match.

In early 2025, Alcaraz had dropped slightly in the rankings to number three. But Alcaraz and his coaching staff were not worried. If anything, the drop in rankings would motivate Alcaraz even more. Alcaraz added another coach to his team, Samuel Lopez. Lopez coached Alcaraz in 2023 when Coach Ferrero had

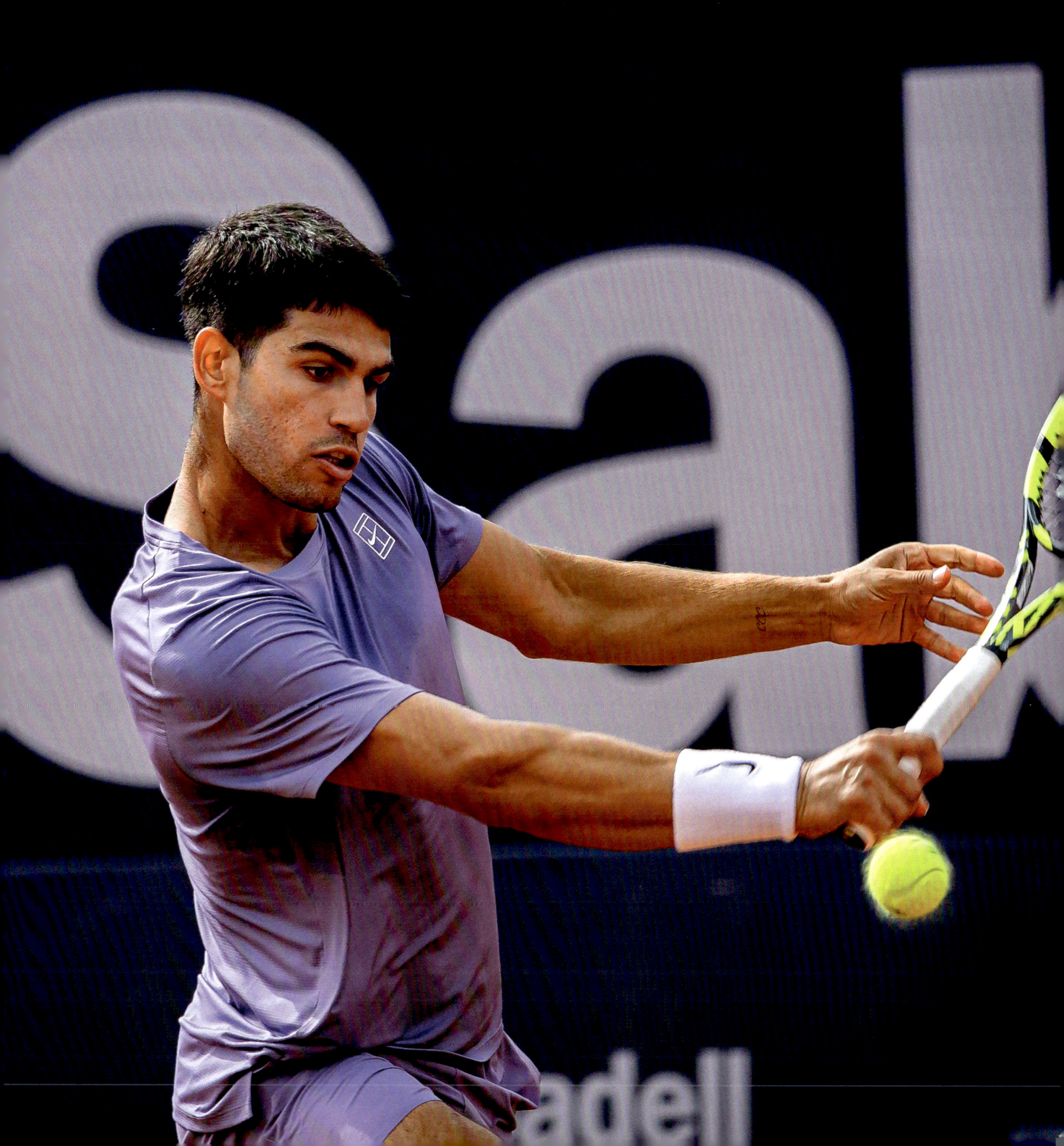

to take a leave. Lopez and Ferrero will work as a team to ensure Alcaraz continues to win.

Not all young people can survive the kind of intense attention that has been placed on Alcaraz over the last few years. But he handles the pressure well and always has a smile on his face. His family helps keep him grounded. Even though he's a millionaire many times over, he still lives with his parents. All three of his brothers play tennis. Jaime is even playing on the competitive tennis circuit.

"I've never wanted to seem like another player, like Federer or Rafa or anyone, I'm just who I am. This is my game."

Every day it seems that Alcaraz gains new fans. Now, a new Netflix docuseries is introducing him to even more people. For *Carlos Alcaraz: My Way,* a camera crew followed Alcaraz for most of

ZOOM IN: THE NEW KING OF TENNIS

Before Alcaraz broke onto the scene, some tennis fans did not know what the future of men's tennis would hold. The three most famous players in recent years were Roger Federer, Nadal, and Djokovic. But Federer had recently retired. Both Nadal and Djokovic were getting older. People were not sure how much longer they could play competitively. Alcaraz seemed to come along at just the right time. He has given the sport a much-needed jolt of new popularity, alongside other up-and-comers like Sinner and Darwin Blanch, who trains with Alcaraz and Coach Ferrero.

2024. It was a big year, with his Wimbledon win and his dramatic Olympic loss. Photos from the docuseries show Alcaraz celebrating his 21st birthday, relaxing on a boat, and smiling with family. The docuseries shows the warm, fun side of Alcaraz that fans do not see on the tennis court.

Alcaraz continues to train at a high level to keep his body and mind in top form. He has matured. When he loses, he no longer throws a tantrum. Even after losses, he talks to reporters and calmly shares with them what he thinks went wrong. But it is after his wins that people see that gigantic, famous smile. He is doing what he loves.

Above all, Alcaraz competes with himself. He wants to be the best version of himself that he can be. If he brings everything to the court during a match, he will be satisfied.

"Every player is different. Every player has their style. And some players will look like other players in the game. But I've never wanted to seem like another player, like Federer or Rafa or anyone," he said. "I'm just who I am. This is my game."

Highlight Reels

SIGNATURE MOVE—THE DROP SHOT

A drop shot is when the ball crosses the net and drops in the opponent's court. It drops so short over the net that it's hard for the opponent to return the ball before it bounces. When Alcaraz was 13 years old, David Ayuela, the captain of the Spanish Junior Davis Cup team at the time, noticed Alcaraz would hit a lot of drop shots. Per match, there might be 20. People would question this. Twenty drop shots? Wait until he became a pro, they thought. He wouldn't be able to do that anymore. But Alcaraz didn't stop his drop shots. During the ATP Tour in the fall of 2024, Alcaraz answered questions from other tennis players. At the time, Sinner, one of Alcaraz's rivals, was ranked No. 1. His recorded question to Alcaraz was, "How can you perform your drop shots in such a beautiful way?" Alcaraz laughed and responded: "I've been practicing the drop shot since I was seven, eight years old. So [I've spent so many] hours on it, that's why." A TikTok video shows Alcaraz telling viewers how to do his drop shot. First, hold the racket in a forehand grip, he explained. Then use the other hand to change to a continental grip. This position allows the player to have backspin with the hit. The player must pretend to hit a forehand but then change the grip at the last second. This way, the opponent doesn't see the shorter shot coming and can't make it on time to return it.

A RIVAL FOR HIS GENERATION

Besides Djokovic, Alcaraz considers Italy's Sinner his rival. Djokovic is sixteen years older than Alcaraz. Alcaraz was born only two years after Sinner. Sinner and Alcaraz turned pro the same year—2018. They're the same generation.

These two young players have similar skills but contrasting styles. For two years, their rivalry had been building, similar to the great rivalry between Federer and Nadal. In 2023, Alcaraz and Sinner played three times, and Alcaraz won all three. Sinner played Alcaraz nine matches by the end of 2024. Alcaraz won five of those. Alcaraz believes he and Sinner will be playing against each other for the next decade at least. As they headed to the Australian Open in January 2025, the talk of their rivalry was noticeable. Sinner had won his first major title the year before at the tournament, which pushed him to the No. 1 spot. He didn't want to lose the title to his Spanish rival. Sinner said, "We usually play high-quality matches because we two players face each other and you bring out your best, the quality of the match usually is very high." The two did not get a chance to face each other: Alcaraz lost to Djokovic in the quarterfinals. Sinner won the tournament.

GIVING BACK

In April 2024 right before the Madrid Open, Alcaraz established a nonprofit called the Alcaraz Foundation, or Fundación Alcaraz. Its mission is to promote health and well-being in children—physical, emotional, and mental. There are three ways the nonprofit wants to help with this mission. They want children to participate in sports. They want children to stay active to improve their physical and emotional health. Finally, they want to help children become aware of problems they might be having in order to overcome them. Alcaraz believes that playing sports provides discipline and fellowship with other children. The foundation encourages "inclusion and well-being in childhood." Alcaraz believes that children should be people before athletes. Just as with the sport itself, the foundation is family focused. Alcaraz is the president, his father is the vice president, and his mother is a member of the board. He has reportedly raised millions for his foundation. Alcaraz helps with other charities, too. For example, Alcaraz signed the pair of sneakers he wore when he won the U.S. Open in 2022 and donated them to Assido, an organization founded in 1981 in Murcia, Spain to help people with Down Syndrome. Each sneaker sold for about $2,500 USD.

Glossary

backhand—a stroke in which the back of the tennis racket makes contact with the ball

backspin—when the ball rotates backwards, or in the opposite direction of where it's going so it moves backward after landing

baseline—the line at the furthest end of the court marking the boundary of play

circuit—an annual group of tennis tournaments that are officially recognized by the professional tennis organizations

continental grip—a neutral grip on the tennis racket taught to beginners

depressurized—tennis balls that do not contain a mixture of air and gas inside; they are often used by beginners

endorsements—when brands or companies pay an athlete to represent their products

forecourt—the area near the net

forehand—a stroke in which the front of the tennis racket makes contact with the ball

match point—when a player needs one more point to win the match

pandemic—the instance of an infectious disease spreading across a country or the world

sponsor—a person or organization that gives financial support to an athlete

tiebreak—a game that is played when the score is 6-6; it decides the winner of the set

underdog—the player who is not expected to win

volley—to hit a ball in the air before it touches the ground

Selected Bibliography

Carayol, Tumaini, "'This boy was born to be No. 1: the making of Carlos Alcaraz." *The Guardian*, May 26, 2023.

"Carlos Alcaraz," *Sports Illustrated*, October 2024.

"Carlos Alcaraz," *Sports Illustrated for Kids*, September/October 2022.

Fendrich, Howard, "Carlos Alcaraz: 19, U.S. Open Champ, No. 1, Unique," The Associated Press, September 12, 2022.

Futterman, Matthew, "Before Carlos Alcaraz Was Great, He Was Good Enough to be Lucky," *The New York Times*, May 28, 2023.

Zagoria, Adam, "Carlos Alcaraz Eyeing Career Slam at Australian Open: 'My Main Goal' For the Season, *Forbes*. January 6, 2025.

Websites

Carlos Alcaraz | Overview
https://www.atptour.com/en/players/carlos-alcaraz/a0e2/overview
News and statistics about Carlos Alcaraz

Carlos Alcaraz Stats, News, Pictures
https://www.espn.com/tennis/player/_/id/3782/carlos-alcaraz
Carlos Alcaraz statistics and biography

Carlos Alcaraz | U.S. Open, Olympics, Results, Biography
https://www.britannica.com/biography/Carlos-Alcaraz
Carlos Alcaraz biography

Index